A SECOND HANDBOOK
OF ETIQUETTE
FOR YOUNG LADIES
AND GENTLEMEN
TO BE USED AS A GUIDE
FOR EVERYDAY
SOCIAL BEHAVIOR

What Do You Do,

Dear?

BY Sesyle Joslin

PICTURES BY Maurice Sendak

A TRUMPET CLUB SPECIAL EDITION

You are in the library reading a book when suddenly you are lassoed by Bad-Nose Bill. "I've got you," he says, "and I'm taking you to my ranch, pronto. Now get moving."

What do you do, dear?

Walk through the library quietly.

You have gone to a tropical island with your friend, the Pirate, to help him find buried treasure. You spend the entire morning digging for it, but then — just as you uncover a large treasure chest — the Pirate's cook rings a bell. "Luncheon is now being served," he says.

What do you do, dear?

Wash your hands before eating.

You are an Indian chief and you invite some cowboys to sit around the fire and smoke the peace pipe. But when it is your turn to puff on the pipe, you accidentally swallow quite a lot of smoke.

What do you do, dear?

Cover your mouth when you cough.

You are one of Robin Hood's merry men and you are sitting in Sherwood Forest reading a good book. Suddenly the Sheriff of Nottingham appears and he says, "I must take you to jail although, forsooth, I am sorry to interrupt you while you are reading."

What do you do, dear?

Find a bookmark to save your place.

You are a brave knight and you are sitting at
the round table with nothing to do because
it is raining. Suddenly the Princess calls you
up. "Prithee, come rescue me," she says.
"It is raining so hard that my castle is
floating away."

What do you do, dear?

Put on your rubbers

before you go out in the rain.

You are at the North Pole, sitting in your igloo eating a bit of blubber, when in comes a huge lady polar bear wearing a white fur coat.

What do you do, dear?

Help her off with her coat.

You are riding downtown in a rather crowded howdah. The elephant stops at the corner and a lady climbs aboard, but there is no place for her to sit.

What do you do, dear?

Offer your seat to the lady.

You are a terrible pirate making a fine lady walk the plank, but when the lady turns to wave farewell to you, she drops her handkerchief.

What do you do, dear?

Pick up the handkerchief and return it to the lady.

You have just taken a great mouthful of pudding when into the dining room rides a handsome prince on a white horse. He says, "I am a handsome prince. Would you care to marry me?"

What do you do, dear?

Swallow what you are eating before you speak.

You are a circus acrobat walking on the high tightwire and you happen to meet a lady tightrope walker coming from the opposite direction.

What do you do, dear?

Step aside and let the lady pass.

You and your friends are at the Princess'
birthday party and everybody is having a
delightful time, only then the footman
announces the unexpected arrival of a large
and hungry dragon.

What do you do, dear?

Remember to thank your hostess for a lovely time.

THIS WAS FOR

Victoria, Alexandra, Julia, and Awich Hine Buff

GRATEFUL ACKNOWLEDGMENT is made to the editors of
the magazine, "Highlights For Children," Columbus,
Ohio, who commissioned the author and artist of
What Do You Say, Dear? to continue their happy
collaboration, which resulted in the episodes
brought together in this book.

Published by The Trumpet Club
666 Fifth Avenue, New York, New York 10103

ISBN 0-440-84983-7

First published by Addison-Wesley Publishing Company
This edition published by arrangement with
HarperCollins Publishers

Printed in the United States of America
January 1993

10 9 8 7 6 5 4 3 2 1
DAN